# INTRUSIVE THOUGHTS AND HAUNTED MUSINGS

## Lucy White

BookLeaf Publishing

India | USA | UK

Intrusive Thoughts and Haunted Musings

© 2021 Lucy White

All rights reserved.



Presentation by BookLeaf Publishing

Web: www.bookleafpub.com

E-mail: info@bookleafpub.com

ISBN: 9789358360585

First edition 2021

1.

Blood is thicker than water

And what poured from my veins when I said that I loved you
was something closer to the consistency of tar

We were caught in the path of an oil slick, desperately
clinging to something that was killing us, choking us, holding
us down

Every time you wrapped your arms around me it felt like a
lifesaver, and I was floating back to shore

But you were just an anchor, weighing me down

Instead of something that should have fuelled us to a better
future,

It drowned us

*2.*

I can feel myself slowly forgetting you with each passing day

The good memories wilted and tainted with a touch of frost

I can feel myself slowly forgetting who I was

"He loves me;

He loves me not"

As each petal falls away, a memory falls with it

"He loves me;

He loves me not"

The fallen petals begin to shrivel and die

Breaking down, decomposing, returning to the earth

I can feel myself slowly forgetting who I am

The sunlight fades as the storm clouds gather

But the rain doesn't wash anything away

It floods the earth and with each flower that falls, the thorns
begin to grow and take their place

3.

They say there's always a calm before the storm.

The waves cease crashing.

The wind is still.

But it's not so much a calm as it is a ceasefire.

When each side lowers their weapons, catches their breath.

Until the next time they fight.

There was a calm between us, too.

We'd shot so many bullets at each other from our trenches that our white flag was little more than a bedsheet.

Shredded and tattered and lifeless, lying between us.

Above the noise.

Above the fighting.

My voice was a whisper that you didn't want to hear.

Stop.

Don't.

I'm tired of fighting.

Aren't you tired of winning.

4.

If I could write a new language to tell you how I feel,

I would.

There aren't enough words in the ones that I speak.

We'd learn it together,

Sharing our favourite phrases and conjugations.

We'd take lessons late into the night when it rains.

We'd have a quick review in the mornings over coffee.

Practice late into the night,

Tangled up in bed sheets and thoughts of each other.

They say it takes 10,000 hours to really master a new skill.

We've barely scratched the surface.

5.

I've always wanted to be artistic and creative.

To paint like Monet.

To sing like Pavarotti.

To write like Shakespeare.

Or Poe.

Or Keats.

When I was growing up I wanted everyone to know my name.

Now I'm older I only want the people I love, to love me.

The people I know, to know me.

Really know me.

I don't need to paint like Monet.

As long as I can paint stars with you, connecting the dots on your back to make constellations and kiss every one of them in our galaxy.

I don't need to sing like Pavarotti.

As long as I can sing whispers of love songs and secrets into your ear when I wake up next to you.

I don't need to write like Shakespeare.

Or Poe.

Or Keats.

As long as one day I can write down our story, our journey, and make a promise and a vow to you.

I don't need anything else.

As long as I'm with you.

6.

In the history books, years from now, they'll talk about world war three.

The war when we faced an invisible enemy.

When no man's land stretched over oceans. Planes were grounded. Highways empty.

Nature came to retake her rightful place in the air, on the land, on sea.

There'll be no winners, no losers, no axis or allies.

Only casualties. Only death. Only statistics.

So many lives ruined with no bloodshed.

The history books will talk about the war of words, politicians hurling accusations across borders.

The history books won't mention me.

But world war three brought me you. If only for a moment. A passing moment.

7.

The Dolmen of Guadalperal lay hidden,

undisturbed,

for millennia until its discovery in 1926.


Spanish Stonehenge kept its secrets for another 50 years until droughts,

and NASA,

uncovered it again.

Just barely skimming the surface of its history like a stone Atlantis,

keeping its 150 orthostats a mystery from the modern world.


70 per cent of the earth is covered in water.

80 per cent of the ocean has never been explored.

Our mysteries,

our histories,

lie in wait for the light to hit them,

for the sun to shine and uncover our deepest secrets,

our darkest desires.

But when the waters recede,

we might see Guadalperal's dolmen again.

8.

It's nights like these, when the rain won't cease, that my thoughts end up tangled in you the way I wish my fingers were tangled in your hair.

It's mornings like this, when I wake with a kiss, in some other man's bed when I wish I was wrapped in your arms instead of wrapped in his sheets.

When the shadows of last night still linger on my fingertips but your name was on the tip of my tongue.

I'd bite down so hard that I'd almost taste blood to keep the whisper of your name out of my mouth.

Even though you're there every minute of every day, I'm barely a ghost in your memory.

You'd think I'd have committed this dance to memory by now


One step forward,

Two steps back


We circle each other, matching the other's intensity and gusto

Waiting for our partner to break into the next move


One step towards recovery,

Two steps towards relapse


And just when I'm ready for the final chorus

The curtain call is early

Casting the stage into darkness

10.

Sometimes fear creeps in through an open window

It seeps in under the cracks under the door

When I least expect it, the shadow of doubt starts to darken

My heart quickens

My blood thickening with every shallow breath

It feels like I'm drowning


Cold, clammy hands reach up and clasp around my throat

My voice is a whisper

A ghost of its former self

The weight of self-doubt pulling me down into the flood of anxiety

Until I'm fading like the last light of day with nothing but darkness stretching out in front of me

11.

It always surprised me when cautionary tales for children
were stripped of their lessons and replaced with aspirations

They both looked the same from the outside

They took the same name

Fairytales


When I was growing up, Ariel gave up her voice and her
family and her home for the love of a man she'd never met

But it worked out

Everything fell into place

She found love and a castle and a place in the world

Rapunzel found love with the man who saved her from the
tower

Snow White and Sleeping Beauty were rescued by their
Prince Charmings


But it was like two sides of the same coin

The good and the bad

And you didn't know which was which until you were in them

Turning the pages of your own story

Unsure if you'd end up in riches or ruins


Now I know that the little mermaid gave up her life, as well as her voice, turning into seafoam when the man chose someone else

Rapunzel let down her hair for a man who left her pregnant and alone

Snow White was the object of every man's affections and objectifications

And Sleeping Beauty was raped in her deep, deep sleep


When I was growing up, I wanted to find my own Prince Charming.

Now I know I did.

I found him on every night out I don't remember,

And every drink that didn't taste quite right in bars that were
too dark, still shone like a chalice in his castle.

My Prince Charmings promised me riches,

Now I see they've ruined me.

12.

I couldn't tell you why I kept trying,

trying,

trying to make him something he wasnt. To make us something we weren't.

Some people have their futures written in the sky,

but we were written in the sensational pages of a tabloid magazine that existed only in my own imagination.

It didn't matter that it wasn't real,

because it was real to me.

But in the end,

when ashes call to ashes and dust calls to dust,

I can call to him and only hear my own echo calling back.

Because he isn't there,

and he never was.

He's in someone else's history book and I'm just left reading an out of date magazine.

13.

Being with you is like being in the eye of a hurricane

A wave of calm washes over me, everything is still

Your eyes are like a dream I can't forget

Whenever I see them I forget to blink

I've stared at them every time I've seen you since we met

Your hands are warm, strong, knowing

They've touched most every part of me

In dreams

In reality

In my bed

Being with you is like being in the eye of a hurricane

The calm before the storm, the high before the low

When the feeling of your hands on my skin replaces the
feeling of his hands on my heart

If only for a moment

A fleeting moment

Being with you is like being in the eye of a hurricane

A disaster waiting to happen

If you were to ask me how I felt I wouldn't have an answer

Just a word we've uttered many times before

Late at night

Drunk on lies and electricity

When hands explored bodies

When heads said no, even though the wine was screaming yes

Being with you is like being in the eye of a hurricane

Every time

The blood reminds you

That you're human

You're alive

You're breathing

It's a reminder

That he didn't break you

They didn't destroy you

You're not alone

15.

There's a stark difference between expectations and reality,

A chasm where relationships go to die.

Observation is the bridge;

Those that see it take the safer pass,

Those that don't are left to fend for themselves, fighting to death for passage.

Living in dreams is easier than facing reality,

When reality means making a choice and dreams make the choice for you.

When perfection has two forms, and both are the wrong choice,

How do you decide which path to choose when both of them lead to destruction?

There's something quite magical about hearing the rain on the window at dawn.

Serene.

Unchanging.

As if nothing in the world exists outside of you and this moment.

Just a subtle splash of water on glass.

Washing away the pain of yesterday.

The mistakes of last night.

A promise between you and the universe to both exist just as you are.

Beautiful.

Fragile.

Perfectly imperfect.

17.

It's a daunting prospect,

giving your heart to someone.

You never know if they'll keep it safe

or break it into a hundred little pieces.

That's what drove him mad in the end,

the beating of that hideous heart.

They always said home was where the heart is.

18.

History has always been told from the perspective of the winners, the victors

The losers only ever get to tell their alternative facts and claim fake news

Live or die, someone else will always be around to tell your story

From Seneca and Pompey, we can take primary documents and still interpret them in different ways with different lenses

Aging eras picked apart piece by piece by people that come generations after

With different ideals and agendas, rewriting a history, a legacy, until it appears more like a fable or a story

We don't get to control every narrative we're part of

Even if you ask to be excluded from the narrative

People will always find a way to write you back in after you wrote your way out

19.

The seasons changing has always brought me a feeling of calm

When the leaves start to fall and the temperature drops, that's when I feel most at peace

It's as though the colder temperatures ease the frost in my chest

When my heart and soul are as cool as the icy chill on the breeze

People around me may shiver and curse the winds that pierce through them

But I float along like the autumn leaves twirling to the ground before winter stakes her claim on the earth

Settling old scores before the rebirth that spring brings into being

www.ingramcontent.com/pod-product-compliance
Lightning Source LLC
La Vergne TN
LVHW010533210726
843508LV00020BA/2961